301 Awesome Facts: Rugby Edition

M.K. Publishing House

Copyright © [2024] by [M.K. Publishing House]

All rights reserved.

No portion of this book may be reproduced in any form without written permission from the publisher or author, except as permitted by U.S. copyright law.

Contents

1. Rugby Rules and Basics — 1
2. Rugby World Cup — 11
3. Legendary Rugby Players — 22
4. Rugby Around the World — 33
5. Cool Rugby Stadiums — 44
6. Rugby in the Olympics — 54
7. Funny Moments in Rugby — 64
8. Rugby Positions Explained — 74
9. Rugby Traditions and Culture — 84
10. Weird and Wonderful Rugby Facts — 94

Chapter One

Rugby Rules and Basics

1. Did you know that in rugby, you can only pass the ball backwards? It's like playing catch, but you have to throw it behind you! This funny rule makes the game super exciting because players have to run forward while tossing the ball back to their friends. It's like a big game of backwards tag!

2. Rugby players score points by putting the ball down in a special area called the "try zone." It's like a touchdown in football, but you actually have to touch the ball to the ground! When a player does this, everyone cheers because they just scored a "try" worth five whole points!

3. In rugby, there's a funny-looking play called a "scrum." It's when players from both teams push against each other like a big group hug, but they're trying to win the ball! The players lock arms and push with all their might. It looks silly, but it's a super important part of the game!

4. Rugby players don't wear helmets or pads like in football. Instead, they wear special shirts called "jerseys" that are super tough and hard to rip. These jerseys have to be strong because other players will grab them during tackles. Some jerseys even have special grip patches to make them easier to hold onto!

5. When a rugby ball goes out of bounds, they don't just throw it back in. Instead, they do something called a "line-out." Players lift their teammates high in the air to catch the ball, like a basketball jump ball, but way cooler! It's like watching acrobats play catch!

6. In rugby, you're not allowed to tackle someone who doesn't have the ball. This rule keeps everyone safe and makes the game fair. It's like playing tag, but you can only tag the person holding the ball. This rule makes players work together to protect their teammate with the ball!

7. Did you know that in rugby, you can kick the ball forward? It's true! Players can kick the ball to move it down the field quickly or to score points. Some players are so good at kicking, they can make the ball soar through the air like a rocket!

8. Rugby has a funny rule called "advantage." If a team breaks a rule, but the other team still has a good chance to score, the referee lets them keep playing! It's like getting a free try at something fun, even if someone else made a mistake.

9. In rugby, there's no blocking allowed. This means players can't stand in the way to protect their teammates. Instead, they have to run alongside them and be ready to catch passes. It's like playing a giant game of keep-away with your friends!

10. When a player gets tackled in rugby, they have to let go of the ball right away. But here's the cool part: the game doesn't stop! Other players can pick up the ball and keep running. It's like hot potato, but with a big oval ball!

11. Rugby has a special kind of kick called a "drop goal." Players can score three points by dropping

the ball and kicking it through the goal posts as it bounces up. It's like kicking a bouncy ball through a giant H-shaped window!

12. In rugby, players can push each other in a "maul." It's like a big group hug that moves! Players gather around the person with the ball and push together to move down the field. It's almost like being a train with lots of cars all pushing forward!

13. There's a cool move in rugby called a "hand-off." When a player with the ball is about to get tackled, they can push the other player away with their free hand. It's like saying "Not today!" and giving a gentle push to keep running.

14. Rugby has a rule called "offside" that's kind of like an invisible line. Players have to stay behind this line when their team doesn't have the ball. If they cross it

too soon, it's like they're cheating at hide-and-seek – they get in trouble!

15. In rugby, there's no time-outs like in other sports. The game keeps going and going! But don't worry, players get a break at halftime. It's like playing a really long game of tag where you only stop once to catch your breath!

16. Did you know that in rugby, you can score points just by kicking the ball through the goal posts? It's called a "penalty kick" or "conversion," and it's worth 2 or 3 points. It's like getting bonus points for being a good kicker!

17. Rugby has a rule that says you can't pass the ball forward, but you can kick it forward! This makes for some exciting plays where players kick the ball ahead and then race to catch it. It's like playing kick-the-can and a race all at once!

18. In rugby, there's a cool move called a "grubber kick." Players kick the ball so it rolls and bounces along the ground. It's like bowling, but with your feet and a rugby ball! This tricky kick can surprise the other team and help score tries.

19. When a player makes a small mistake in rugby, the other team gets a "free kick." This means they can kick the ball without anyone trying to stop them. It's like getting a free throw in basketball, but you use your feet instead of your hands!

20. Rugby has a rule that says players must stay on their feet when they're trying to get the ball. No diving allowed! It's like playing a game where the floor is lava, and you have to stay standing to keep playing.

21. In rugby, there's a funny thing called a "ruck." When a player gets tackled, other players gather around and try to push each other away from the

ball. It looks like a bunch of kids fighting over the last cookie, but it's all part of the game!

22. Did you know that in rugby, you're allowed to lift your teammates? During line-outs, players can lift their friends high in the air to catch the ball. It's like being a cheerleader and a football player all at once!

23. Rugby has a cool rule about kicking the ball out of bounds. If you kick it out from inside your own half of the field, the other team gets to throw it in where it went out. But if you kick it from your own half and it bounces out in their half, you get to throw it in! It's like getting a bonus for a really good kick.

24. In rugby, there's no blocking allowed when you don't have the ball. This means players have to be really sneaky to get open for passes. It's like playing hide-and-seek while running around – you have to be clever to find open spaces!

25. Rugby has a rule that says you can't tackle someone in the air. If a player jumps to catch the ball, you have to wait until they land before tackling them. It's like giving someone a safe zone while they're playing hot lava monster!

26. Did you know that in rugby, you can score a try by touching the ball to the goal post? If a player is being tackled near the goal, they can reach out and touch the ball to the padded part of the post to score. It's like playing tag with a giant pole as home base!

27. Rugby has a special kick called a "up-and-under" or "box kick." The kicker kicks the ball high in the air so their teammates have time to run under it and catch it. It's like playing catch with yourself, but your friends get to join in!

28. In rugby, there's a rule that says you can't throw the ball into the crowd on purpose. If you do, the

other team gets the ball. It's like having to keep the ball in bounds during a game of catch, even when you're excited about scoring!

29. Rugby has a cool rule about tackling. You have to use your arms to wrap around the other player when you tackle them. No shoulder charges allowed! It's like giving someone a big bear hug, but they're trying to run away from you.

30. Did you know that in rugby, the game doesn't end when the clock runs out? Play continues until the ball goes out of bounds or a team scores. It's like having bonus time in a video game – the excitement keeps going until the very last second!

Chapter Two

Rugby World Cup

1. The Rugby World Cup is like a big party for rugby teams from all over the world! It happens every four years, just like the Olympics. Teams from different countries come together to play lots of exciting matches. It's like a huge playground game, but with grown-ups playing and millions of people watching!

2. Did you know the Rugby World Cup trophy is called the Webb Ellis Cup? It's named after a boy who, legend says, picked up the ball during a soccer game and ran with it, creating rugby! The cup is super shiny and gold-colored. Winners get to hold it up high and feel like superheroes!

3. The first-ever Rugby World Cup happened in 1987. That's a long time ago - maybe when your parents were kids! New Zealand and Australia hosted it together, like throwing a big sports party with their neighbor. New Zealand's team, the All Blacks, won that first tournament. They were like the first-ever world champions of rugby!

4. At the Rugby World Cup, teams play in colorful uniforms called jerseys. Each country has its own special colors. For example, New Zealand wears all black, which is why they're called the All Blacks! It's

like a big dress-up party where everyone wears their country's favorite colors.

5. The Rugby World Cup has a special song called the World in Union. It's like the tournament's theme song! Fans from all over the world sing it together before big matches. Imagine your whole school singing the same song at once - that's what it's like!

6. In the Rugby World Cup, teams are divided into groups, kind of like teams in your class for a project. They play against other teams in their group first. The best teams from each group then go on to play in the knockout stages. It's like a big tournament in your school playground!

7. The Rugby World Cup isn't just for boys - there's a Women's Rugby World Cup too! It started in 1991 and is just as exciting. The women players are super strong and fast, showing that girls can be amazing

rugby stars too. It's like having two awesome birthday parties instead of one!

8. During the Rugby World Cup, some players become famous for their special moves. Like Jonah Lomu from New Zealand, who was so big and fast, he ran through other players like a truck! He became a rugby superhero that kids everywhere wanted to be like.

9. The Rugby World Cup has a mascot, just like your school might have! In 2019, the mascot was a cool lion named Ren-G. Having a mascot is like having a fun, imaginary friend that everyone at the tournament can cheer for and take pictures with!

10. At the end of each Rugby World Cup, players from different teams swap jerseys. It's like trading your favorite toys with friends! This shows good sportsmanship and helps players remember the fun

they had, even if they didn't win. It's like getting a souvenir from a new friend!

11. The Rugby World Cup has been played in many different countries. It's like the tournament goes on a big world tour! From England to Japan, and even New Zealand, it's traveled to more places than most people do in their whole lives. It's like a globe-trotting adventure for rugby!

12. During the Rugby World Cup, fans do special cheers for their teams. New Zealand fans do the Haka, a traditional Maori war dance. It's super loud and a bit scary! Imagine your whole class doing a special dance to cheer on your school team - that's what it's like!

13. The Rugby World Cup ball is a special shape - not round like a soccer ball, but oval! It's designed to be easier to catch and run with. The official ball for

each World Cup has a unique design. It's like getting a new, cool-looking ball for every big tournament!

14. In the Rugby World Cup, some matches can end in a tie. When this happens in knockout stages, they play extra time. If it's still tied, they have a kicking contest! It's like playing a game, then playing some more, and if you still can't decide the winner, you have a special tie-breaker!

15. The Rugby World Cup has seen some amazing comebacks! In 2015, Japan beat South Africa in a huge upset. It was like if a small school's team beat the big city champions! Everyone was so surprised and excited, it became one of the most famous matches ever.

16. During the Rugby World Cup, host cities decorate their streets with flags and banners. It's like the whole city is having a big rugby party! Imagine if

your whole town was decorated for your birthday - that's how exciting it looks during the World Cup!

17. The Rugby World Cup final is watched by millions of people around the world. It's like if everyone in a huge city sat down to watch the same TV show at the same time! The excitement is so big, you can almost feel it through the TV screen.

18. In the Rugby World Cup, teams sing their national anthems before each match. It's like a big music show before the game starts! Players stand in a line and sing really loud and proud. Sometimes, they even cry because they're so happy to represent their country!

19. The Rugby World Cup has a special countdown clock that starts four years before the tournament. It's like having the world's longest countdown to a

birthday party! This clock helps everyone get excited and ready for the big event.

20. During the Rugby World Cup, there's a special ceremony to welcome teams to the host country. It's like getting a big, friendly hello when you visit someone's house! Each team gets a special welcome that includes local traditions and sometimes even gifts.

21. The Rugby World Cup trophy travels around the host country before the tournament starts. It's like a famous rock star going on tour! People can see it up close and even take pictures with it. Imagine your favorite toy becoming super famous and going on a trip around the country!

22. In the Rugby World Cup, there's a special award called the "Player of the Tournament." It's like being named the most valuable player in your school sports day, but for the whole world! This player gets a

shiny trophy and becomes super famous in the rugby world.

23. During the Rugby World Cup, many countries have special coins or stamps made to celebrate. It's like getting a cool sticker book, but the stickers are actually money or can be used to send letters! These become treasures that people keep to remember the exciting tournament.

24. The Rugby World Cup has its own special language! Words like "try," "scrum," and "ruck" might sound funny, but they're important rugby words. It's like learning a secret code that all rugby fans understand. You can impress your friends by learning these words!

25. At the Rugby World Cup, there's a special ceremony to open and close the tournament. It's like the first and last day of school, but way more excit-

ing! There are fireworks, music, dancing, and all the teams parade around in their uniforms. It's a super colorful and fun show!

26. During the Rugby World Cup, some matches are played in huge stadiums that can fit as many people as a small town! Imagine if your whole school, plus all your families, plus all your neighbors filled a giant playground - that's how big these stadiums are!

27. The Rugby World Cup has seen some really long matches! If teams are tied after extra time, they keep playing until someone scores. The longest match lasted 100 minutes! That's like playing through two whole recess times without stopping!

28. In the Rugby World Cup, teams can bring special good luck charms. Some teams have lucky mascots or wear lucky socks. It's like having your favorite

teddy bear with you for a big test - these charms help players feel brave and strong!

29. During the Rugby World Cup, the host country sometimes teaches visiting fans about their culture. It's like having an extra fun social studies class! Fans might learn new dances, try new foods, or learn to say "Hello" in a new language while enjoying the rugby.

30. After winning the Rugby World Cup, the champion team gets to keep the Webb Ellis Cup for four years. It's like borrowing a trophy from your school for a really long time! They have to take good care of it and bring it back for the next tournament, all shiny and ready for a new winner.

Chapter Three

Legendary Rugby Players

1. Jonah Lomu was like a superhero in rugby! He was so big and fast that other players bounced off him when they tried to tackle him. Imagine a giant teddy bear running super fast with a rugby ball -

that's what Jonah was like! He scored lots of tries and made people love watching rugby.

2. Richie McCaw was the captain of New Zealand's All Blacks team for a long time. He played so many games that if you counted them in days, it would be like he played rugby non-stop for almost two weeks! He was like a superhero leader who always knew how to win.

3. Dan Carter could kick the rugby ball so well, it was like he had magic feet! He could make the ball fly between the goal posts from really far away. Imagine being able to kick a ball over your house - that's how good Dan was! He scored more points than any other rugby player ever.

4. Jonny Wilkinson was famous for kicking with his "wrong" foot! He practiced so much that he could kick equally well with both feet. It's like being able

to write perfectly with both hands. Jonny won the World Cup for England with a super important kick in 2003!

5. Brian O'Driscoll was so good at rugby, people called him "BOD" - like he was a superhero! He played for Ireland and was amazing at running with the ball and scoring tries. Brian was like a magician on the field, always doing unexpected things to surprise the other team.

6. Serge Blanco was a French player who ran so fast and smoothly, people said he was like water flowing down a river. He could find gaps in the other team that no one else could see. Imagine being able to run through a crowd without bumping into anyone - that's how good Serge was!

7. David Campese was an Australian player who invented a special move called the "goose-step." It made

him look like he was dancing while running with the ball! Other players found it super hard to catch him. It was like he had springs in his shoes!

8. Gareth Edwards played rugby a long time ago, but people still say he was one of the best ever! He could do everything well - run, kick, and pass. Imagine being the best at every game in the playground - that's what Gareth was like in rugby.

9. Martin Johnson was so tall and strong, he was like a friendly giant on the rugby field! He was the captain when England won the World Cup in 2003. Martin was like the boss of a superhero team, telling everyone what to do to win the game.

10. Zinzan Brooke was a big player who could do things that usually only smaller players could do. He could run fast, pass well, and even kick goals! It was

like seeing an elephant being as graceful as a ballerina. Zinzan surprised everyone with his amazing skills.

11. Michael Jones was so good at tackling other players, people called him "The Iceman"! He could stop anyone running with the ball. Michael was like a superhero with freezing powers, cooling down the other team's hot moves and keeping them from scoring.

12. Jason Robinson was small for a rugby player, but he was super fast! He could change direction so quickly that other players got confused. It was like he had invisible roller skates that could turn on a dime. Jason scored amazing tries that made crowds go wild!

13. Joost van der Westhuizen was a South African player who could pass the ball super far and accurately. It was like he had a magic wand instead of hands!

Joost could send the ball flying to his teammates even when other players were trying to stop him.

14. John Eales was so good at everything in rugby, people called him "Nobody" - because "Nobody's perfect"! He was tall and could jump really high to catch the ball. John was like a giraffe who could leap like a kangaroo, amazing everyone with his skills.

15. Siya Kolisi has an amazing story - he grew up poor in South Africa but became the captain of their national team! He led South Africa to win the World Cup in 2019. Siya is like a real-life superhero, showing kids that they can achieve big dreams.

16. Portia Woodman is one of the best women's rugby players ever! She's super fast and can score lots of tries. Portia is like a rocket on the field - zoom, zoom, zoom, and she's scored again! She shows that girls can be amazing rugby superstars too.

17. Maggie Alphonsi was so good at tackling, people called her "The Machine"! She helped England's women's team win lots of games. Maggie was like a friendly robot on the field, programmed to stop the other team from scoring no matter what!

18. Jonny Wilkinson practiced kicking so much, he made little dents in his parents' garage door! He would kick the ball for hours and hours. It's like if you practiced writing your name a million times - you'd become the best name-writer ever!

19. Dan Carter once scored 33 points in one game against the British and Irish Lions. That's more points than some whole teams score! It's like if you scored all the goals in a soccer game by yourself. Dan was like a one-man team sometimes!

20. Brian O'Driscoll scored 47 tries in international games. That's like scoring a touchdown in every

football game for four whole seasons! He was so good at finding ways to score, it was like he had a map of the field that no one else could see.

21. Richie McCaw played in 148 international games. That's more than any other rugby player ever! It's like if you played in every single game at school for years and years. Richie was like the Energizer Bunny of rugby - he just kept going and going!

22. George Gregan played for Australia 139 times! He was so good at passing the ball, it was like he had eyes in the back of his head. George could always find his teammates, even if they were hiding. He was like a rugby magician!

23. Phaidra Knight was so strong and fast, she could play many different positions in rugby. It's like being able to play every instrument in a band! Phaidra

showed that you can be good at lots of different things if you work hard.

24. Kieran Read was amazing at catching the ball when it was kicked high in the air. It was like he could fly! Kieran would jump up and grab the ball, even with other players trying to catch it too. He was like a superhero with the power to leap tall buildings!

25. Shane Williams was one of the smallest professional rugby players, but he was super fast! He could run around other players like they were standing still. Shane was like a little race car zooming past big trucks on a highway.

26. Emily Scarratt is so good at kicking and running with the ball, she's like a Swiss Army knife of rugby! She can do everything well. Emily has helped England win lots of games. She's like a superhero with many different powers!

27. Faf de Klerk has crazy curly blonde hair that bounces when he runs! He's small but super tough and isn't afraid of bigger players. Faf is like a bouncy, curly-haired rugby superhero who proves that you don't have to be big to be great at rugby.

28. Israel Folau could jump so high to catch the ball, it looked like he was flying! He was amazing at catching high kicks. Israel was like a kangaroo playing rugby, bouncing higher than everyone else to grab the ball out of the sky.

29. David Pocock was so good at stealing the ball from other teams, it was like he had sticky hands! He could grab the ball away even with lots of other players around. David was like a rugby ninja, appearing out of nowhere to take the ball.

30. Beauden Barrett is so fast, he once scored a try in just 13.2 seconds! That's quicker than it takes to tie

your shoelaces. Beauden is like The Flash of rugby, zooming past other players before they even know the game has started.

Chapter Four

Rugby Around the World

1. Rugby is played in lots of countries, like a big global game of tag! From snowy Canada to sunny Australia, people everywhere love chasing the oval ball. It's like having friends to play with all around

the world. Imagine if your playground game could be played by kids in every country!

2. In New Zealand, rugby is super popular! It's like their national treasure. Kids there grow up playing rugby like you might play hide and seek. The New Zealand team is called the All Blacks, and when they do their special dance called the Haka before games, it's scarier than any Halloween costume!

3. In Wales, rugby is so loved that some people say it's like a religion! On game days, everyone wears red shirts and sings really loud songs together. It's like if your whole town had a big, noisy party every time your school team played. The dragon on their flag almost comes alive with excitement!

4. In Fiji, they play a lot of rugby on the beach. Imagine playing your favorite sport with soft sand under your feet and blue waves nearby! Fijian players

are known for being really good at a type of rugby called "Sevens," where they run super fast and do tricky moves.

5. In South Africa, winning the Rugby World Cup in 1995 was a big deal for the whole country. It helped bring people together after some tough times. It was like when you make up with your best friend after an argument, but for a whole nation! Rugby became a symbol of unity.

6. In Argentina, they love rugby so much that their national team is nicknamed "Los Pumas." But they don't really look like pumas - it was a mistake! Someone thought the animal on their logo was a puma, but it was really a jaguar. It's like calling your pet cat a lion by accident!

7. In Japan, rugby is getting more and more popular. They even hosted the World Cup in 2019! It was like

throwing a big rugby party and inviting the whole world. Japanese fans are super polite - they clean up the stadium after games, even if their team loses!

8. In Georgia, they play a traditional game called "Lelo burti" that's a bit like rugby. Whole villages play against each other trying to get a ball to their side. It's like a giant game of tug-of-war, but with a ball! This old game helped make rugby popular in Georgia.

9. In Madagascar, rugby is one of the most popular sports! It's surprising because Madagascar is an island far from where rugby started. It's like if your favorite food came from a country you've never visited. They love rugby so much, it's almost as popular as soccer!

10. In England, where rugby was invented, they have a famous stadium called Twickenham. It's so big it

can fit 82,000 people! That's like having every kid in 100 schools all watching a game together. It's nicknamed "The Cabbage Patch" because it used to be a farm!

11. In France, they have a saying: "Rugby is a sport for thugs played by gentlemen." It means that even though rugby looks rough, the players are very polite. It's like having a mud fight but saying "please" and "thank you" the whole time!

12. In Australia, they play both rugby union and rugby league. It's like having two favorite flavors of ice cream! The rugby union team is called the Wallabies, named after a jumping animal a bit like a kangaroo. Imagine a team of bouncing players!

13. In Tonga, a tiny island country, rugby is huge! Their national team is called "Ikale Tahi" which means Sea Eagles. When they play, it's like the

whole country stops to watch. Imagine if your whole school took a break to watch you play your favorite game!

14. In Scotland, they play rugby in a stadium called Murrayfield that has its own ghost! People say they've seen a man in old-fashioned clothes wandering around. It's like having a friendly spooky mascot for your team. Don't worry, he's said to bring good luck!

15. In Italy, rugby is growing more popular every year. They call it "rugby" but pronounce it differently, like "roob-gee." It's like learning a new language just for sports! Italian rugby fans are known for being very passionate and singing loud songs during games.

16. In Canada, they play rugby even when it's snowing! Sometimes they have to shovel the field before

they can play. It's like building a snowman and playing your favorite sport at the same time. Canadian rugby players must be extra tough to play in the cold!

17. In Samoa, a small island country, rugby is so important that some of their money has rugby players on it! Imagine if your allowance had pictures of your favorite sports stars. Samoan rugby players are known for being really strong and fast.

18. In Ireland, both the Republic of Ireland and Northern Ireland play on the same team. It's like if two classes that usually do everything separately came together to make one super team for a big game. Their team symbol is a shamrock, a lucky three-leaf clover.

19. In Kenya, rugby sevens is super popular. It's a faster version of rugby with fewer players. Kenyan players are known for being really fast runners. It's

like they have superspeed! Their team is called "Shujaa," which means "heroes" in Swahili.

20. In Romania, they call rugby players "stejarii," which means "oaks." It's because rugby players are strong like big oak trees! Imagine a whole team of walking, talking trees playing rugby. That's how tough Romanian rugby players seem!

21. In the United States, rugby is growing more popular every year. Some people call it "football without pads." It's like playing your favorite video game but on hard mode! More and more schools are starting rugby teams.

22. In Sri Lanka, they've been playing rugby for over 100 years! They even play it in some schools instead of homework (just kidding, they still have homework). Sri Lankan rugby is known for being really fast and exciting, like a game of super-speed tag.

23. In Portugal, rugby is not as popular as soccer, but it's growing! They call their national team "Os Lobos," which means "The Wolves." Imagine a pack of friendly wolves playing rugby together. Portuguese players are known for being clever and quick.

24. In Russia, rugby is played even in the really cold parts of the country. Sometimes the ball is so cold it feels like an ice cube! Russian rugby players must be extra brave to play when it's freezing outside. It's like having a snowball fight but with a rugby ball.

25. In Uruguay, they love rugby so much that they call it "the game played by gentlemen." Uruguayan rugby players are known for being really polite, even when they're tackling each other! It's like saying "excuse me" before tagging someone in a game of tag.

26. In Namibia, a country in Africa, rugby is one of the most popular sports. They have to be careful of

wild animals sometimes wandering onto the rugby fields! Imagine playing your favorite game and seeing a giraffe watching from the sidelines.

27. In Hong Kong, they have a famous rugby tournament every year. Teams from all over the world come to play. It's like having a big international party where the game is rugby! The stadium is so noisy and exciting during this tournament, it's like a big rock concert.

28. In Chile, rugby is becoming more popular, especially in schools. Chilean rugby players are known for being really tough and never giving up. It's like if the Little Engine That Could was a rugby team! They keep trying even when things are hard.

29. In Spain, they sometimes call rugby "el rugby" or "balón oval" which means "oval ball." Spanish rugby is known for being really passionate and exciting. It's

like a big, sporty fiesta every time there's a game! Players celebrate tries by waving their arms like matadors.

30. In the Netherlands, they play rugby even though their country is very flat and sometimes below sea level! They have to be careful the rugby fields don't get too wet. It's like playing your favorite sport in a giant bathtub! Dutch players must be good swimmers too.

Chapter Five

Cool Rugby Stadiums

1. Twickenham Stadium in England is so big, it could fit 82,000 people! That's like having every kid in 100 schools watching a game together. It's nicknamed "The Cabbage Patch" because it used to be a farm. Imagine playing rugby where cabbages once grew - that's pretty cool!

2. Eden Park in New Zealand is famous for being really loud! When fans cheer, it sounds like a giant roar. The stadium is named after a person, not a garden. It's like if your school named its playground after your principal! The All Blacks hardly ever lose games here.

3. Millennium Stadium in Wales has a roof that can close! It's like a giant umbrella for the whole stadium. When it's closed, the cheering gets even louder because the sound bounces around inside. Imagine playing in a big, noisy bubble - that's what it's like!

4. Ellis Park in South Africa is so high up, it's hard for visiting teams to breathe! It's like playing on top of a mountain. The air is thinner up there, so players get tired faster. Home team players are used to it, though - it's like they have superpowers!

5. Suncorp Stadium in Australia has a cool nickname - "The Cauldron." It's because the stadium keeps all the noise and excitement bubbling inside, like a giant cooking pot! The crowd is so close to the field, it feels like they're part of the game.

6. Murrayfield in Scotland is said to have its own ghost! Some people say they've seen a man in old-fashioned clothes walking around. Don't worry, he's friendly! It's like having a spooky mascot. Maybe he's just a big rugby fan who never wants to leave!

7. Stade de France in Paris is so fancy, it has heated seats for some lucky fans! It's like sitting in a comfy armchair while watching the game. The stadium looks like a giant spaceship from the outside. Imagine aliens landing to watch a rugby match!

8. Principality Stadium in Wales has such steep seats, it feels like you're looking down from a skyscraper!

The top seats are so high, they have their own nickname - "The Gods." It's like watching the game from a cloud! But don't worry, every seat has a great view.

9. Forsyth Barr Stadium in New Zealand has a see-through roof! It lets sunlight in but keeps rain out. It's like playing in a giant greenhouse. The grass can grow naturally inside, so it's always green and perfect for rugby, even in winter!

10. Aviva Stadium in Ireland looks like a giant shiny bowl from the outside! Its curved shape makes it look like a spaceship. At night, it lights up in different colors. It's like having a giant nightlight for the whole city of Dublin!

11. ANZ Stadium in Australia was built for the Olympics, but now it's great for rugby too! It's so big, you could fit 4 jumbo jets inside it. Imagine

playing rugby on an airplane runway - that's how big this stadium feels!

12. Newlands Stadium in South Africa is one of the oldest rugby stadiums in the world! It's been around since your great-great-grandparents were little. Playing there is like stepping back in time. The stadium has a beautiful view of mountains nearby.

13. Allianz Stadium in France looks like a big, colorful bubble! Its roof changes colors at night, like a giant mood ring. It can be blue, red, or green depending on which team is playing. It's like the stadium is cheering along with the fans!

14. FMG Stadium Waikato in New Zealand has seats so close to the field, fans can almost touch the players! It's like watching the game from your front yard. The stadium is shaped like a big bowl, so the cheering echoes and gets super loud.

15. Thomond Park in Ireland is famous for being really quiet during kicks. Fans stay so silent you could hear a pin drop! It's like playing in a giant library. But when someone scores, it suddenly gets as loud as a rock concert!

16. Stade Mayol in France has a cool tradition. Players touch a statue of a coconut seller for good luck before games! It's like having a magic good luck charm for the whole team. The stadium is right next to the sea, so you can smell the salty air during games.

17. Sapporo Dome in Japan has a pitch that slides in and out of the stadium! It's like a giant drawer. The grass field moves outside to get sunlight, then slides back in for games. It's like magic - now you see it, now you don't!

18. Estadio Charrua in Uruguay is named after a Native American tribe. It's like playing in a history

lesson! The stadium isn't very big, but it's known for having really passionate fans. It's proof that you don't need to be big to be awesome!

19. Lansdowne Road in Ireland was the world's oldest international rugby stadium until it was rebuilt. It was so old, some seats were made of wood! Playing there was like traveling back in time. Now it's all new and shiny, but still full of history.

20. Hong Kong Stadium hosts a famous rugby tournament every year. During this time, it's like the whole city turns into one big rugby party! The stadium is in the middle of tall buildings, so it looks like the skyscrapers are watching the game too.

21. Fiji's National Stadium is surrounded by palm trees! It's like playing rugby on a tropical island - because it is! The weather is usually hot, so sometimes

they use sprinklers to cool down the field. It's like having a water park and a rugby field in one!

22. Estádio Universitário in Portugal is part of a university. It's like if your school playground was a famous sports stadium! Students can watch international rugby matches and then go straight to class. Talk about a cool school!

23. Mbombela Stadium in South Africa has seats that look like zebra stripes! From above, the whole stadium looks like a giant zebra. It's in an area where you can see real zebras and giraffes nearby. Imagine wild animals watching you play!

24. Estadio Nacional Complutense in Spain is part of a university too. It's so old, it's like playing in a history book! The stadium has seen lots of important games and events. It's like a grandpa of rugby stadiums, with many stories to tell.

25. Richardson Stadium in Canada sometimes has to deal with snow! They have to clear the field before games in winter. It's like building a snow fort and a rugby field at the same time. Canadian rugby players must be part snowman!

26. National Stadium in Singapore has a roof that can open and close in just 20 minutes! It's like a giant eyelid blinking. The stadium also has special cooling systems to keep everyone comfortable in the hot weather. It's like playing in a big, comfy fridge!

27. Samoa's National Stadium is right next to the ocean! You can hear the waves during the game if it's quiet enough. It's like playing rugby on a beach, but with a proper field. Sometimes the salty air makes the ball a bit slippery!

28. Stade Maurice David in France is in a city famous for art. The stadium itself looks like a piece of art! It

has big, colorful shapes on the outside. It's like playing rugby inside a giant painting. Maybe it inspires players to make their game look beautiful too!

29. Estadio Elias Figueroa Brander in Chile is named after a famous soccer player, but it's great for rugby too! It's near the ocean and mountains, so you get amazing views while watching the game. It's like playing in a postcard!

30. Aerports de Paris Stadium in France is under construction and will have a wooden roof! It'll be the biggest wooden structure in the world. It's like playing under a giant treehouse. The stadium will even have its own forest around it!

Chapter Six

Rugby in the Olympics

1. Rugby was first played in the Olympics way back in 1900! That's so long ago, your great-great-grandparents might not have been born yet. It was like adding a new flavor to an ice cream shop - everyone was excited to try it out!

2. In the early Olympic rugby games, teams could have as many players as they wanted! Imagine playing tag with 100 kids on each team. It would be super crowded and crazy! Now, they have rules about how many players can be on each team.

3. The USA won the first-ever Olympic gold medal in rugby! It's like winning first place in a big school contest. They beat France in the final game. The funny thing is, most Americans didn't even know how to play rugby back then!

4. Rugby disappeared from the Olympics for a long time - 92 years! That's like waiting for your birthday to come around 92 times. It must have been so exciting when it finally came back in 2016. It was like reuniting with a long-lost friend!

5. When rugby came back to the Olympics in 2016, it was a different kind of rugby called "Rugby Sevens."

It's like regular rugby but faster and with fewer players. Imagine if your favorite board game suddenly had new, exciting rules!

6. In Olympic Rugby Sevens, each team only has seven players on the field. That's less than half of a regular rugby team! It's like playing soccer with just a goalie and two other players. This makes the game super fast and exciting!

7. Rugby Sevens games in the Olympics are really short - only 14 minutes long! That's shorter than most TV shows. It's like if your recess was super quick, but packed with fun. Players have to score as many points as they can in this short time.

8. Fiji won their country's first-ever Olympic medal in 2016, and it was gold in Rugby Sevens! Imagine if your school won a big prize for the very first time -

everyone would be so happy and proud! The whole country of Fiji celebrated like it was a huge party.

9. In the Olympics, both men and women play Rugby Sevens. It's like having two awesome parties at the same time! Both tournaments are equally exciting, and fans cheer just as loud for the women's teams as they do for the men's.

10. Australia's women's team won the first Olympic gold medal in Women's Rugby Sevens in 2016. They were like superheroes, making history! Imagine being the first person ever to do something - that's how these players felt.

11. Olympic rugby players are super fast! Some can run 100 meters in less than 11 seconds. That's faster than a car driving in a parking lot! It's like having a superpower that makes you zoom across the field.

12. In Olympic Rugby Sevens, if a team scores a try (like a touchdown in football), they get 5 points! Then, they get to kick the ball for 2 more points. It's like getting extra candy for finishing your dinner - a sweet bonus!

13. The Rugby Sevens field in the Olympics is the same size as a regular rugby field, but with fewer players. It's like having a huge playground all to yourself! Players have lots of space to run around and do cool moves.

14. Some countries that aren't usually great at other Olympic sports are really good at Rugby Sevens! It's like being the best at one subject in school, even if you struggle with others. Countries like Fiji and New Zealand are Rugby Sevens superstars!

15. In the 2016 Olympics, the Rugby Sevens matches were played in a stadium that looks like a giant

seashell! It's called Deodoro Stadium. Imagine playing your favorite sport inside a magical seashell - that's what it was like for the rugby players!

16. Rugby players at the Olympics don't wear any protective gear except a mouthguard. No helmets or pads! It's like playing tag without wearing your coat - they must be very brave and careful not to get hurt.

17. If a Rugby Sevens match is tied at the end of normal time in the Olympics, they play extra time. The first team to score any points wins! It's like a sudden-death round in a video game - super exciting and nerve-wracking!

18. Some Olympic Rugby Sevens players also compete in other sports! It's like being good at playing the piano and the guitar. For example, some athletes have switched between Rugby Sevens and sprinting or bobsledding!

19. In the Olympics, if a player gets in trouble, they might be sent to the "sin bin." It's like a timeout corner in your classroom, but on a sports field! Players have to sit out for 2 minutes, which is a long time in a short game.

20. The Rugby Sevens ball used in the Olympics is smaller than a regular rugby ball. It's like using a mini-version of your favorite toy. This smaller ball makes it easier for players to pass and run with it really fast!

21. During Olympic Rugby Sevens games, teams switch sides at halftime. It's like a big game of musical chairs, but with rugby teams! This makes sure that neither team has an unfair advantage from wind or sun.

22. Some countries have special nicknames for their Olympic Rugby Sevens teams. For example, the

New Zealand men's team is called the "All Blacks Sevens." It's like having a cool superhero name for your sports team!

23. In the Olympics, Rugby Sevens games have no breaks except for halftime. It's like playing a game at recess without stopping - you have to be super fit! Players run non-stop for two 7-minute halves.

24. The referee in Olympic Rugby Sevens uses a whistle just like in other sports, but they also use special hand signals. It's like the referee is doing a fun dance to tell everyone what's happening in the game!

25. In the 2021 Tokyo Olympics (held in 2022 due to COVID-19), fans weren't allowed in the stadium to watch Rugby Sevens. It must have felt like playing in a giant empty classroom! But people all over the world watched on TV and cheered from home.

26. Some Olympic Rugby Sevens players can kick the ball so high, it looks like it's going to the moon! It's called an "up-and-under" kick. Imagine kicking a ball so high that it disappears into the clouds before coming back down!

27. In Olympic Rugby Sevens, players don't have set positions like in regular rugby. Everyone has to be good at everything! It's like being in a school play where you have to know all the parts, not just your own.

28. The Olympic Rugby Sevens tournament happens over just three days! It's like having a super-fast sports camp. Teams might play several games in one day, so they have to be ready for lots of action.

29. In the Olympics, if a Rugby Sevens player makes a mistake, the other team gets a "free kick." It's like getting a free turn in a board game because someone

else broke a rule. This can lead to exciting, quick changes in the game!

30. The next Olympic Rugby Sevens tournament will be in Paris in 2024! Players are already practicing hard for it. It's like getting ready for a big test, but the test is playing an awesome sport in front of the whole world!

Chapter Seven

Funny Moments in Rugby

1. Once, a player's shorts fell down during a tackle! He kept running with the ball, trying to hold his shorts up with one hand. It was like having a wardrobe malfunction in the middle of a game of

tag. Everyone was laughing so hard, they almost forgot about the game!

2. In a match in England, a streaker (someone who runs on the field with no clothes) was tackled by a player! It was like an extra game of tag that nobody expected. The naked person thought he was sneaky, but the rugby player was sneakier!

3. During a game in New Zealand, a seagull flew onto the field and stole the ball! It tried to fly away with it, but the ball was too heavy. It was like watching a bird play rugby. The players had to wait for the seagull to get bored and fly away!

4. Once, a player scored a try (like a touchdown) and got so excited, he did a backflip! But he landed on his face instead. Oops! It was like trying to do a cool dance move and tripping over your own feet. His teammates couldn't stop giggling!

5. In a rainy game, a player slid to score a try but went right past the try line and into a big puddle! He looked like he was taking a bath in his uniform. It was like having a water slide on the rugby field - fun, but very wet!

6. During a windy match, a player tried to kick the ball, but the wind blew it backwards! It went over his head and his team lost yards. It looked like the ball was playing a trick on him. Mother Nature scored a point that day!

7. Once, a player's fake tan came off on another player's white shorts during a tackle! It looked like the player with white shorts sat in orange paint. They both got up looking very confused, like they'd just shared a magical orange crayon.

8. In a muddy game, two teams got so dirty that no one could tell them apart! The referee had to stop the

game so they could change shirts. It was like a big, messy game of mud pies where everyone was on the same brown team!

9. A player once celebrated scoring by jumping into the crowd, but he forgot there was a barrier! He bounced off and fell back onto the field. It was like trying to jump into a swimming pool and hitting the water with a big splash!

10. During a game, a player's boot came off, so he threw it to the sideline. But it hit the referee on the head! The ref wasn't hurt, but he looked very surprised. It was like an accidental game of dodgeball in the middle of rugby!

11. Once, a player tried to make a big kick, but he slipped and fell on his bottom! The ball dribbled forward just a tiny bit. It looked like he was doing a

funny dance move instead of playing rugby. Everyone laughed, even his own team!

12. In a windy game, a player's hair gel wasn't strong enough! His hair kept blowing in his face, making it hard to see. He looked like a sheep dog trying to play rugby. His teammates kept telling him which way to run!

13. During a match, a player accidentally tackled the referee, thinking he was on the other team! The ref ended up with a muddy uniform too. It was like a game of tag where even the person calling "time out" gets caught!

14. Once, a player tried to catch the ball but it got stuck in his jersey! He ran around with the ball hidden, and no one knew where it was. It was like a magic trick in the middle of the game - now you see it, now you don't!

15. In a rainy game, a player slid to catch the ball but kept sliding... right off the field and into a big puddle! He came up looking like he'd been swimming. It was like having an unexpected water park visit during the match!

16. During a game, a bird pooped on a player's head just as he was about to catch the ball! He was so surprised, he missed the catch. It was like nature was playing a silly prank on him. His teammates couldn't stop laughing!

17. Once, two players from the same team accidentally tackled each other! They both thought the other had the ball. It looked like they were dancing instead of playing rugby. Their coach must have been very confused!

18. In a muddy game, a player got tackled and came up with a mud mustache! He looked like he'd grown

a beard in just a few seconds. His teammates called him "Mud Face" for the rest of the game.

19. During a match, a player's jersey ripped so much it looked like a cape! He ran around looking like a superhero playing rugby. His teammates started calling him "Captain Rugby" for the rest of the game.

20. Once, a player tried to kick the ball, but his boot flew off instead! The boot went further than the ball would have. It was like his shoe decided it wanted to play rugby too. Everyone watched the boot soar through the air!

21. In a game, a player caught the ball and ran the wrong way! His teammates were yelling at him to turn around. It was like playing a board game and moving your piece backwards by mistake. He was very red-faced when he realized!

22. During a lineout (when players lift each other to catch the ball), a player's shorts got caught and ripped! He had to play the rest of the game with a big hole in his pants. It was like having a wardrobe malfunction in front of everyone!

23. Once, a player tried to dive dramatically to score a try, but the ground was super muddy. He ended up sliding way past the try line, looking like a human slip-n-slide! His white uniform turned completely brown.

24. In a windy game, the referee's whistle blew away! He had to chase it across the field while all the players watched. It was like a funny game of catch in the middle of the rugby match.

25. During a match, a player's mouthguard flew out when he yelled. It landed on another player's head and stuck there! It looked like the other player had

grown a colorful horn. Everyone was laughing too hard to keep playing for a minute.

26. Once, a player tried to kick the ball, but it hit the goalpost and bounced back, hitting him on the head! It was like the ball was playing a game of boomerang. His teammates teased him about having a hard head for the rest of the game.

27. In a televised match, a camera operator got too close to the action and a player accidentally tackled him! The poor camera person got a surprise rugby lesson. It was like being in the game without meaning to be!

28. During a game, a dog ran onto the field and started chasing the ball! The players had to stop and try to catch the dog. It was like having an unexpected game of fetch in the middle of a rugby match.

29. Once, a player celebrated scoring a try by doing a cartwheel, but he got dizzy and fell over! He looked like a wobbly top spinning on the field. His teammates laughed and helped him up, still cheering for the score.

30. In a muddy game, two players tackled each other and slid so far they ended up in a big puddle outside the field! They came up looking like swamp monsters. It was like they decided to go swimming instead of playing rugby!

Chapter Eight

Rugby Positions Explained

1. The Fullback is like the last superhero defender! They stay at the back of the field and catch high kicks. Imagine being the final boss in a video game - that's the Fullback! They need to be brave and have

super-catching skills to stop the other team from scoring.

2. Wing players are the speed demons of rugby! They run super fast along the sides of the field to score tries. It's like being the fastest kid in a race at school. Wings need to be quick as lightning and able to dodge other players like they're playing a giant game of tag.

3. Centers are the middle players who are good at everything! They run fast, tackle hard, and pass the ball well. It's like being the kid in class who's great at math, reading, AND sports. Centers need to think quickly and be ready for anything, just like a superhero!

4. The Fly-half is like the team's brain! They make important decisions about where to pass or kick the ball. Imagine being the captain of a pirate ship,

telling everyone where to go - that's the Fly-half! They need to be smart and have magical kicking skills.

5. Scrum-halves are like the postmen of rugby! They pass the ball out from scrums and rucks. It's like being the kid who passes out worksheets in class - everyone depends on you! Scrum-halves need to be quick thinkers and have super-fast hands.

6. Flankers are the troublemakers of rugby! Their job is to tackle opponents and steal the ball. It's like being the sneakiest player in a game of capture the flag. Flankers need to be strong, fast, and not afraid to get dirty!

7. The Number 8 is like a Swiss Army knife player! They can do a bit of everything - run with the ball, tackle, and help in scrums. Imagine having every su-

perpower at once - that's the Number 8! They need to be strong, fast, and good at making decisions.

8. Props are the strong protectors in rugby! They hold up the scrum and stop the other team from pushing through. It's like being the strongest kid on the playground who can hold the door shut when everyone's pushing. Props need to be super strong and brave!

9. The Hooker has a funny name but an important job! They throw the ball into lineouts and try to win it in scrums. It's like being the best at playing "Monkey in the Middle" - you're always in the center of the action! Hookers need strong arms and perfect aim.

10. Locks are the tall trees of rugby! They jump high to catch the ball in lineouts. Imagine being so tall you could touch the ceiling - that's a Lock! They also

push hard in scrums. Locks need to be tall, strong, and good at jumping.

11. The Fullback is also like a rocket launcher! They can kick the ball really far to help their team get out of trouble. It's like having a super-strong kick in kickball. Fullbacks need to have powerful legs and be good at aiming their kicks.

12. Wings don't just run fast - they're also acrobats! They often have to jump and twist in the air to score tries in the corner. It's like being a gymnast and a sprinter at the same time. Wings need to be flexible and have amazing balance.

13. Centers are like the bouncers of rugby! They stop the other team's attacks by tackling hard. Imagine being a human wall that no one can get past - that's what Centers do! They need to be brave and have shoulders like rocks.

14. The Fly-half is also the team's sharpshooter! They kick for goals to score extra points. It's like being the best at throwing paper into the trash can from across the room. Fly-halves need to have nerves of steel and super-accurate kicking.

15. Scrum-halves are the noisiest players on the field! They shout instructions to their team all the time. It's like being the loudest singer in the school choir. Scrum-halves need to have big voices and not be shy about bossing their friends around!

16. Flankers are like rugby vacuum cleaners! They clean up loose balls all over the field. Imagine being able to spot a tiny crumb on a huge floor - that's what Flankers do with rugby balls! They need eagle eyes and quick hands.

17. The Number 8 is the back of the bus in scrums! They control the ball at the base and decide when to

pick it up. It's like being the last person in a conga line who decides where everyone goes. Number 8s need to be smart and make good choices.

18. Props are like sumo wrestlers in rugby! They use their weight to push in scrums and rucks. Imagine being so strong you could push a car - that's what Props do! They need to eat lots of vegetables to stay big and strong.

19. The Hooker is the team's best thrower! They throw the ball straight in lineouts. It's like being the best at playing darts, but the dart is a big rugby ball! Hookers need to practice throwing perfectly straight every day.

20. Locks are the team's basketball players! They get lifted up to catch the ball in lineouts. Imagine playing basketball, but your teammates lift you up

instead of you jumping - that's what Locks do! They need to not be afraid of heights.

21. Fullbacks are also the last line of defense! If they miss a tackle, the other team might score. It's like being the goalie in soccer - there's no one behind you to save the day. Fullbacks need to be brave and never give up!

22. Wings are like cheetahs on the rugby field! They can run super fast to score tries. Imagine being able to run faster than a car - that's how quick Wings are! They need to practice running every day to stay speedy.

23. Centers are the team's bulldozers! They run straight and hard to break through the defense. It's like being a human bowling ball, knocking down all the pins. Centers need to be strong and not afraid to bump into people.

24. The Fly-half is the team's chess master! They think of clever plays to outsmart the other team. It's like being the smartest kid in class, but for sports. Fly-halves need to study the game and always be thinking of new ideas.

25. Scrum-halves are like the team's spark plugs! They start most of the plays and keep the game moving. Imagine being the first domino that makes all the others fall - that's the Scrum-half! They need to be full of energy all the time.

26. Flankers are the team's ninjas! They appear out of nowhere to make tackles or steal the ball. It's like being the best at hide-and-seek, but in a sports game. Flankers need to be sneaky and quick.

27. The Number 8 is like the team's truck driver! They pick up the ball from the scrum and drive forward. Imagine pushing a heavy shopping cart really

fast - that's what the Number 8 does! They need to be strong and able to run while carrying the ball.

28. Props are the team's anchors! They keep the scrum steady and strong. It's like being the roots of a big tree, holding everything in place. Props need to have strong legs and never get pushed around.

29. The Hooker is the team's fishing expert! They try to "hook" the ball back in scrums. Imagine playing a claw machine game at an arcade, but with your foot - that's what Hookers do! They need to have clever feet.

30. Locks are the team's power plants! They provide most of the power in scrums and mauls. Imagine being a human forklift, pushing heavy things around - that's what Locks do! They need to eat lots of energy food to stay strong.

Chapter Nine

Rugby Traditions and Culture

1. The Haka is a famous rugby tradition from New Zealand. It's a special dance the All Blacks team does before each game. Imagine your whole class doing a scary dance to frighten the other team! The players

stamp their feet, stick out their tongues, and shout loud words. It's like a big, noisy warm-up!

2. In rugby, players shake hands with the other team after the game. It's like saying "good game" to everyone you played tag with at recess. No matter who wins or loses, players show good sportsmanship. It's a way of saying, "We had fun playing with you!"

3. Rugby has a funny tradition called "earning your jersey." New players on a team might get a plain jersey without a number. They have to work hard and play well to earn their number! It's like leveling up in a video game - the more you play, the cooler your character looks!

4. Many rugby teams have special songs they sing together after winning a game. It's like having a victory dance, but with singing! Players link arms and sing

loudly in the locker room. Imagine your whole class singing your school song after acing a big test!

5. In rugby, there's a tradition called the "third half." It's when both teams hang out together after the game to eat and chat. It's like having a big picnic with your friends after playing in the park. Players who were tackling each other earlier become friends off the field!

6. Some rugby players grow big mustaches during special tournaments. It's called Movember, and it helps raise money for men's health. Imagine if all the boys in your class grew silly mustaches for a month! It's a fun way to support a good cause.

7. In Wales, rugby is so popular that some people say it's like a religion! On game days, everyone wears red shirts and sings really loud songs together. It's like if

your whole town had a big, noisy party every time your school team played.

8. Rugby has a tradition called "capping." When a player first represents their country, they get a special cap. It's like getting a gold star for doing something amazing! Players keep these caps forever to remember their special day.

9. In rugby, there's a tradition of respecting the referee. Players call the referee "Sir" or "Ma'am" and never argue with them. It's like how you respect your teacher in class. This helps keep the game fair and friendly, even when it gets rough!

10. Some rugby stadiums have funny nicknames. For example, Twickenham in England is called "The Cabbage Patch" because it used to be a vegetable farm! Imagine playing your favorite sport in a giant garden. It makes the stadium sound extra special!

11. In South Africa, they blow on a funny horn called a vuvuzela during rugby games. It makes a loud "VOOOO" sound! Imagine if your whole class had noisy trumpets to blow during a school assembly. It would be super loud but lots of fun!

12. Rugby has a tradition called the "Guard of Honor." After a big game, players from both teams make two lines and clap as the winning team walks through. It's like making a tunnel of high-fives for your friends who just won a race!

13. In rugby, players often swap jerseys after international games. It's like trading your favorite t-shirt with a new friend from another country! Players keep these jerseys as special souvenirs to remember the game and their opponents.

14. Some rugby clubs have funny eating traditions for new players. They might have to eat a raw onion

or a really hot chili! It's like a silly food challenge you might do at a birthday party. Don't worry, it's all in good fun!

15. In rugby, there's a tradition of giving your opponent three cheers after the game. Everyone lines up and shouts "Hip hip hooray!" three times. It's like giving a round of applause to your friends after putting on a great play.

16. Many rugby teams have a mascot, just like your school might have! Some are funny animals or characters that dance around during the game. Imagine if your favorite stuffed animal came to life and cheered for your team!

17. In some countries, people have big rugby parties called "rugby sevens." It's like a carnival with lots of games, but the main event is watching quick rugby

matches! People dress up in silly costumes and have fun all day long.

18. Rugby has a tradition called the "clubhouse." After games, players from both teams go to a special room to hang out and talk. It's like having a playdate with the kids you just played against! This helps players become friends off the field.

19. In New Zealand, little kids play a version of rugby called "Rippa Rugby." Instead of tackling, they pull tags off each other's waists. It's like playing flag football but with a rugby ball! This helps kids learn rugby in a safe and fun way.

20. Some rugby players have a tradition of wearing special underwear or socks for good luck! It's like having a lucky pencil you always use for tests. They think these special clothes will help them play better.

21. In Wales, there's a famous rugby song called "Bread of Heaven." Thousands of fans sing it together at games. Imagine if your whole school knew a special song and sang it super loud to cheer on your team!

22. Rugby has a funny tradition called the "boat race." It's not really a boat race, but a game where teams compete to drink water really fast! It's like having a contest to see who can finish their milk first at lunch, but for grown-ups.

23. In some places, there's a tradition of playing rugby on the beach! Imagine playing your favorite sport with soft sand under your feet and waves nearby. It's like mixing a beach day with a sports day!

24. Rugby players often have nicknames for each other. Sometimes these names are silly or based on funny things that happened. It's like how you might

call your friend "Giggles" if they laugh a lot. These nicknames make being on the team extra fun!

25. In rugby, there's a tradition of having a team dinner the night before a big game. It's like having a special family meal before an important day at school. Players eat together and talk about their game plan.

26. Some rugby fans have a tradition of wearing funny hats to games. They might wear hats that look like their team's mascot or in their team's colors. Imagine if everyone in your class wore silly hats for a day - that's what it looks like in the stands!

27. In rugby, there's a tradition called the "centurion." When a player plays 100 games for their country, they become a centurion. It's like becoming a superhero in the rugby world! These players get special honors and lots of cheers from fans.

28. Rugby has a tradition of giving funny names to plays. There might be a play called "Bomb Squad" or "Cheese Grater." It's like having secret code names for your plans in a game of spies. These names make remembering plays more fun!

29. In some rugby clubs, new players have to stand on a chair and sing a song in front of everyone. It's like show-and-tell, but with singing! This helps new players feel part of the team, even if they feel a bit shy at first.

30. Rugby has a tradition called the "tour." Teams travel to other countries to play games and learn about different cultures. It's like going on a school trip, but for sports! Players get to make friends from all over the world and try new foods.

Chapter Ten

Weird and Wonderful Rugby Facts

1. Did you know that the first rugby ball was actually pig's bladder wrapped in leather? Yucky! Imagine playing with a balloon made from a pig. It was bouncy but smelly! Today, rugby balls are made of rubber

and leather, much nicer to play with and they don't smell like bacon!

2. The longest game of rugby ever played lasted 24 hours and 30 minutes! That's longer than a whole day! It was played in Northern Ireland for charity. Imagine playing your favorite game from breakfast time one day until breakfast time the next day. The players must have been super tired!

3. In rugby, the referee is sometimes called the "whistleblower." It's not because they tell secrets! It's because they blow a whistle to start and stop play. Imagine if your teacher used a whistle instead of their voice in class. It would be noisy but fun!

4. The Rugby World Cup trophy is called the Webb Ellis Cup. But here's the funny part - Webb Ellis didn't really invent rugby! He's part of a made-up story about picking up a soccer ball and running

with it. It's like naming a prize after a fairy tale character!

5. There's a type of rugby played in water called "underwater rugby." Players wear snorkels and fins and try to score goals in baskets at the bottom of a pool. It's like mixing rugby with swimming and basketball all at once. Imagine playing your favorite sport while holding your breath!

6. The heaviest rugby player ever weighed 467 pounds! That's as heavy as a baby elephant. His nickname was "The Refrigerator" because he was so big. Imagine trying to tackle someone as big as your fridge - it would be like hugging a building!

7. In Japan, they have a rugby-playing robot! It can run with the ball and even kick it. Imagine playing rugby against a team of friendly robots. It would be

like a sci-fi movie come to life! The robot isn't as good as human players yet, but it's still super cool.

8. There's a rugby team in Finland that plays on ice! They wear special shoes with spikes to avoid slipping. Imagine playing your favorite sport on an ice rink. It's like mixing rugby with ice skating. The players must be very careful not to fall!

9. The rugby term "try" comes from "try at goal." Originally, you didn't get points for touching the ball down - it just gave you a "try" at kicking a goal! Imagine if in basketball, you had to throw the ball through the hoop twice to score. Rugby has changed a lot since then!

10. There's a special rugby ball that lights up in the dark! It has LED lights inside that make it glow. Imagine playing rugby at night with a glowing ball. It would be like playing with a star that fell from the

sky! This ball helps people play rugby even when it's dark outside.

11. The oldest rugby club in the world is called Guy's Hospital RFC. It was formed in 1843. That's so long ago, your great-great-great grandparents might not have been born yet! Imagine playing on a team that's been around for over 175 years. It's like being part of living history!

12. In Wales, there's a rugby pitch (field) that's on a slope. One end is 12 feet higher than the other! Imagine playing on a field that's like a slide. Running one way would be super easy, but the other way would be like running up a hill. Players must have very strong legs!

13. The rugby scrum was invented because of a rule that said the ball couldn't be picked up if it was on the ground. Players would gather around and try to

kick it to their teammates. Imagine if you had to play soccer without using your hands - that's how rugby started!

14. There's a type of rugby played on sand called "beach fives." It's played with five players on each team. Imagine playing your favorite sport at the beach. You'd get to enjoy the sun and waves while scoring tries! But running in sand is much harder than on grass.

15. The shortest international rugby player was just 5 feet tall! His nickname was "Pocket Rocket" because he was small but super fast. Imagine someone the size of a big kid in your class playing against adults. It shows that in rugby, size isn't everything!

16. In rugby sevens, games are only 14 minutes long! That's shorter than most TV shows. Imagine if your recess was a rugby game - it would be over before you

know it! But don't worry, they play lots of games in one day to make up for it.

17. There's a rugby ball that can tell you how far and fast it's been thrown! It has a computer chip inside. Imagine if your toys could tell you how high you threw them or how fast you ran with them. It's like having a smart rugby ball!

18. The rugby posts used to be shaped like an H, but with no crossbar. Players would argue about whether the ball went over or not. Imagine playing basketball with just the poles and no hoop - it would be hard to tell if you scored! That's why they added the crossbar.

19. In 1973, a rugby game was played at the top of Mount Everest! It was the highest altitude game ever played. Imagine playing your favorite sport on top of the tallest mountain in the world. The air would

be so thin, it would be hard to run and catch your breath!

20. There's a rugby ball that can float on water! It's made with special foam inside. Imagine playing catch in a swimming pool with a ball that doesn't sink. You could have rugby practice and swim time all at once! It's perfect for beach or pool parties.

21. The longest successful kick in rugby was 110.6 yards! That's longer than a whole football field. Imagine kicking a ball from one end of your school to the other. The player who did this must have had super strong legs!

22. In some rugby games, they use a pink ball instead of the usual white one. It's to support breast cancer awareness. Imagine playing with a ball that looks like bubblegum! It's a fun way to make people think about an important cause while enjoying the game.

23. There's a version of rugby played on trampolines! It's called Bossaball. Players bounce around trying to get the ball over a net. Imagine mixing rugby with volleyball and bouncy castles. It looks super fun but also very tricky to play!

24. The rugby ball is sometimes called a "quanco." This funny name comes from the company that first made rubber bladders for the balls. Imagine if your toy was named after the factory that made it. It's like calling your teddy bear "Stuffing Factory"!

25. In wheelchair rugby, players use special chairs with bumpers, like little car bumpers. They bump into each other to make tackles! Imagine playing bumper cars but as a sport. It shows that everyone can play rugby, even if they use a wheelchair.

26. There's a rugby team in England called the Vampires! Don't worry, they don't bite. They just play

at night because their players work during the day. Imagine having soccer practice at midnight. It would be like being on a team of superheroes with secret identities!

27. The first rugby game in the Olympics had 3 teams! France played two games in one day to decide the winner. Imagine having a three-way game of tag. It would be crazy but fun! Now Olympic rugby is more normal, with just two teams playing each other.

28. There's a rugby ball that makes noises when you kick it! It squeaks or whistles depending on how you kick it. Imagine playing with a ball that talks back to you. It would be like having a funny robot as part of your game!

29. In some rugby clubs, new players have to bite the head off a raw fish! Don't try this at home. It's a silly

tradition to welcome new team members. Imagine if you had to eat something yucky to join a club at school. Rugby players must be very brave!

30. The biggest rugby scrum ever had 1,297 people! It looked like a giant group hug on the field. Imagine if your whole school got together to make one big scrum. It would be like a massive game of sardines where everyone squishes together!

31. There's a type of rugby played in the mud called "swamp soccer." Players get super dirty while trying to score. Imagine playing your favorite sport in a giant mud puddle. You'd need a long bath afterward, but it would be so much fun!

Printed in Great Britain
by Amazon